The Double-Slash Dilemma

Dilemma

The Inventor's Regret in Web History

Authored by
Zahid Ameer

Published by

Goodword eBooks

DEDICATION

"I dedicate this book to my beloved parents, whose wisdom I hold in the highest regard. Their every word of guidance has been a beacon of light, illuminating the path of my life and shaping the essence of who I am."

The Double-Slash Dilemma

Contents:

The Double-Slash Dilemma

Introduction: The Birth of the World Wide Web

In 1989, a monumental shift in human history began, though few people realized it at the time. At CERN, the European Organization for Nuclear Research, a British scientist named Tim Berners-Lee was quietly working on a project that would transform the world in unimaginable ways. Berners-Lee wasn't driven by profit or fame, but by a need to solve a problem that scientists and researchers were increasingly facing—how to share information seamlessly and efficiently across the globe. What emerged from this pursuit was the World Wide Web, an invention that fundamentally altered the way we connect, communicate, and conduct business.

Before the creation of the web, the internet already existed in a basic form, connecting networks of computers across long distances. However, it was a fragmented, specialized system used by government agencies, military personnel, and researchers. It lacked a cohesive, user-friendly structure that would allow anyone, anywhere, to access and share information freely. Berners-Lee's genius lay in recognizing the need for a unifying system, one that could harness the power of the internet and make it accessible to the masses.

Tim Berners-Lee's Vision: A Web of Interconnected Documents

Berners-Lee's breakthrough came in the form of hypertext, a concept that allowed text to be linked to other documents. The idea wasn't new—researchers had been experimenting with hypertext systems since the 1960s. However, it was Berners-Lee who realized that hypertext could be used to link documents over the internet, creating a vast, interconnected "web" of information. In March 1989, he proposed a system for sharing and managing information over computer networks. His concept involved three main technologies that are still the foundation of the web today: **HTML (Hypertext Markup Language)**, **URI/URL (Uniform Resource Identifier/Locator)**, and **HTTP (Hypertext Transfer Protocol)**.

HTML was the language that enabled the creation of web pages; URLs provided the addresses that allowed users to locate those pages; and HTTP was the protocol that allowed for the transfer of information between computers. Together, these technologies formed the architecture of the web as we know it.

In 1990, Berners-Lee developed the first web browser and editor, which he called **WorldWideWeb**. It ran on a NeXT computer, and its purpose was to allow users to browse and edit documents stored on computers anywhere in the world. By Christmas of that year, Berners-Lee had successfully implemented the first website, a simple page explaining what the World Wide Web was and how it worked. This marked the quiet birth of what would become the most transformative communication platform in history.

From Niche Tool to Global Infrastructure

The early web was a modest, academic tool primarily used by researchers at CERN. Berners-Lee's vision, however, was far more expansive. He imagined a world where the web was not confined to elite institutions, but open and accessible to anyone with a computer. In 1991, the first website went live to the public, and in the following years, the World Wide Web Consortium (W3C) was founded by Berners-Lee to set standards for web development, ensuring that the web would remain a universal and open medium.

The web spread rapidly in the early 1990s, thanks in part to the release of popular web browsers like **Mosaic** and **Netscape Navigator**, which made it easier for non-experts to navigate this new digital landscape. What had once been a tool for researchers quickly became a global phenomenon, transforming industries ranging from publishing to commerce to entertainment. By the mid-1990s, companies like Amazon and eBay were beginning to explore e-commerce, revolutionizing how people shopped and did business. Media companies began streaming content online, and search engines like Yahoo! and Google emerged, changing the way we accessed and organized information.

The Power and Impact of a Simple URL

At the heart of this revolution was the humble URL—the Uniform Resource Locator. It was the address system Berners-Lee created to allow users to find information on the web. A URL typically started with **"http://"** followed by a domain name (such as "www.example.com"), which would direct the user to the specific web page they were trying to access.

In the design of the URL, Berners-Lee made a small, almost unconscious decision that he would later come to regret: the inclusion of the double slashes **"//"** after the **"http:"** portion of the address. In programming, the double-slash was a common convention used to indicate comments or a special function, and in the early days of web development, it seemed natural to include it in the URL structure. At the time, the addition of the slashes didn't seem significant, especially when the web was still small, and there were far fewer addresses to type or manage.

However, as the web grew, so did the recognition that these two extra characters were largely unnecessary. In a 2009 interview, Berners-Lee humorously reflected on this decision, admitting that the double slashes served no real purpose in the URL format. If he had left them out, he noted, it would have saved a great deal of time and space over the years, given how many billions of URLs were being typed daily across the globe.

The Double-Slash Dilemma: A Minor Mistake, a Major Impact

While the double slashes might seem like an insignificant detail, it points to a larger truth about the creation of the World Wide Web: even the smallest design decisions can have far-reaching consequences. Berners-Lee's regret over the double slashes underscores the complexity of web design and the unpredictable ways that technologies evolve.

At the time, the inclusion of the slashes was a logical choice based on the programming conventions that Berners-Lee and his peers were familiar with. The fact that they became a minor inconvenience for billions of web users worldwide was an unintended consequence of a system that, in almost every other way, functioned flawlessly.

This book, **The Double-Slash Dilemma: The Inventor's Regret in Web History**, delves into this fascinating story, exploring the technical, cultural, and historical significance of Tim Berners-Lee's invention. The decision to include the double slashes serves as a lens through which we can examine the broader process of innovation, highlighting how even the most ingenious creations are subject to the whims of human imperfection.

The Broader Significance of Small Choices in Design

Berners-Lee's minor regret opens up a discussion about how small design decisions can impact technology over time. When we think of the internet today, we often focus on its vastness, its speed, and its ability to connect every corner of the globe in an instant. However, what made this possible were the tiny, detailed choices that went into its construction—choices like the creation of HTML, the structure of URLs, and the adoption of HTTP as the primary protocol for web communication.

The inclusion of the double slashes is a reminder that even the most advanced technologies are shaped by human hands and minds. Designers and engineers work with the knowledge and tools available at the time, often unaware of the lasting implications of their choices. What may seem trivial in one era can become a defining feature—or flaw—in the next. As the web evolved, it became clear that

Berners-Lee's small oversight was an inconvenience, but it also became an emblem of the complexity and creativity behind one of the most significant inventions of the 20th century.

A Deep Dive into Web History

In this book, we'll trace the story of the World Wide Web from its inception to its explosive growth and eventual domination of global communication and commerce. We'll explore how Berners-Lee's vision came to life and how his decisions—both large and small—shaped the modern internet. The inclusion of the double slashes is just one part of a larger narrative that illustrates the power of innovation and the often unpredictable consequences of technological progress.

Along the way, we'll dive into the technical details of the web's architecture, the cultural shifts it sparked, and the incredible impact it has had on the world. From the early days of static web pages to today's dynamic, interactive, and interconnected digital ecosystems, the web's evolution is a story of creativity, collaboration, and constant reinvention.

The Double-Slash Dilemma: The Inventor's Regret in Web History will provide readers with a comprehensive understanding of how the World Wide Web came to be, how it transformed society, and how even the smallest

The Double-Slash Dilemma

design decisions can echo through history. The story of the double slashes is, in many ways, the story of the web itself—a tale of brilliance, ambition, and the ongoing quest to make the world a more connected place.

Chapter 1: Tim Berners-Lee and the Genesis of the Web

The creation of the World Wide Web is one of the most transformative technological achievements of the 20th century. At its core, the story is one of necessity meeting innovation, driven by the vision and ingenuity of Tim Berners-Lee, a British computer scientist. His work at CERN (the European Organization for Nuclear Research) in the late 1980s laid the foundation for a revolutionary change in how we access, share, and interact with information.

CERN in the 1980s: The Need for a New System

In the 1980s, CERN was a hub of scientific research. Home to some of the most brilliant minds in physics and engineering, it played a crucial role in cutting-edge experiments, particularly in the field of particle physics. However, while CERN's research output was groundbreaking, the infrastructure for sharing information was inefficient and fragmented. Scientists from around the globe needed a reliable system to exchange data, collaborate on projects, and share their findings with one another. This need for information sharing was a

13

significant challenge. While the internet already existed in a basic form, largely serving as a network to connect computers, it lacked a cohesive method for linking documents and enabling easy access to the vast amounts of information stored on different machines.

At the time, Berners-Lee worked as a software engineer at CERN, and he observed firsthand the frustrations faced by researchers. They were drowning in data, and though various systems had been devised to organize information, none were universally compatible. Different computers and different systems used different file formats, making the exchange of information cumbersome and time-consuming.

Berners-Lee, seeing an opportunity to streamline the way information was shared, began to formulate a plan to unify these disparate systems. He envisioned a world where any document, located anywhere, could be accessed through a common, interconnected structure. This would be done using *hypertext*—a concept that allowed one document to reference another through links. Although hypertext wasn't a new idea (it had been discussed and experimented with since the 1960s), no one had successfully applied it to the growing network of interconnected computers.

The Early Vision: "Information Management: A Proposal"

In March 1989, Berners-Lee submitted a formal proposal to CERN, titled **"Information Management: A Proposal"**. In this document, he outlined his vision for what would later become the World Wide Web. His proposal aimed to create a decentralized system that could store and retrieve information in a way that allowed researchers to navigate easily between different resources. It wasn't just about transferring data; it was about making connections between pieces of information. He described it as a "web" of information, where documents could be linked, providing a dynamic and user-friendly way to access knowledge.

Initially, the proposal was met with skepticism. Many of his colleagues at CERN couldn't grasp the magnitude of what Berners-Lee was suggesting, viewing it as overly ambitious and unnecessary. At that time, there were simpler solutions for file sharing that didn't involve creating an entirely new system. However, Berners-Lee's vision wasn't just about solving an immediate problem—it was about creating a framework that would continue to expand as the internet grew.

In collaboration with Robert Cailliau, a fellow CERN engineer, Berners-Lee revised and refined his proposal. By

1990, the idea began to gain traction, and they secured funding from CERN to develop a prototype.

Building the World Wide Web: HTML, HTTP, and URLs

The World Wide Web as we know it today is built on three essential technologies that Berners-Lee developed in rapid succession:

1. **HTML (HyperText Markup Language)** – HTML is the language used to create and structure web pages. It allows text to be formatted, images to be embedded, and links (hyperlinks) to be created between documents. HTML was the foundation of the web, giving creators the ability to build interlinked documents that could be easily navigated.
2. **HTTP (HyperText Transfer Protocol)** – HTTP is the protocol that governs the communication between a client (such as a web browser) and a server. It specifies how requests for web pages are made and how servers respond to those requests. HTTP made it possible for computers to exchange information across the web.
3. **URL (Uniform Resource Locator)** – URLs are the addresses of web resources. Every web page, image,

or document on the web has a unique URL that allows users to locate and access it. The structure of URLs includes several components, including the protocol (e.g., "http"), the domain name (e.g., "example.com"), and the specific path to the document.

Together, these three innovations formed the backbone of the World Wide Web.

Launching the First Web Browser: WorldWideWeb

In 1991, Tim Berners-Lee completed the development of the first-ever web browser, which he named *WorldWideWeb*. Unlike modern browsers, which focus primarily on viewing web pages, WorldWideWeb was a full-fledged editor. Users could not only browse web pages but also create and edit them. This was in line with Berners-Lee's vision of a collaborative web, where anyone could contribute information.

The first version of the web browser ran on NeXT computers (a computing platform created by Steve Jobs after leaving Apple). It provided a graphical interface for navigating the web, allowing users to click on hyperlinks to move between documents. The web had officially been born, and while it was rudimentary compared to what we use today, it represented a major leap forward in how information could be shared.

At first, the web was primarily used within CERN, but Berners-Lee made the software freely available to the world, ensuring that it could be adopted and expanded by a global audience. This decision to keep the web open and free was a critical factor in its rapid expansion.

The Creation of the URL and the Double-Slash Dilemma

One of the key components of the web's functionality was the Uniform Resource Locator, or URL. URLs are what allow us to navigate the web, identifying the location of specific documents and resources. The format of the URL was a crucial decision, as it would determine how users accessed content across the web.

In designing the URL, Berners-Lee opted to include several elements:

- The protocol (e.g., "http"), which specifies how the web browser should communicate with the server.
- The domain name (e.g., "example.com"), which identifies the server where the document is located.

- The path, which specifies the exact location of the file on the server.

However, Berners-Lee made one choice that would later cause him to express regret: the inclusion of the double-slashes ("//") after the protocol ("http:").

At the time, this made sense to Berners-Lee because it followed established conventions in programming and file paths, where slashes were used to denote directories. It was a logical extension of the systems that already existed in other areas of computing. However, as the web grew in size and scope, the double slashes became an unnecessary part of the URL structure. They served no functional purpose, but they were replicated in billions of URLs, typed by users all over the world.

In 2009, Berners-Lee reflected on this decision and admitted that, in hindsight, he regretted including the double slashes. He noted that their absence would have made URLs cleaner and saved time, space, and effort across the billions of web addresses typed into browsers. It was a small but significant choice that exemplified the unforeseen consequences of decisions made in the early days of the web.

The Impact of the World Wide Web

The Double-Slash Dilemma

Though the double-slash dilemma might seem trivial in the grand scheme of things, it highlights the power of design choices in shaping the digital world. The World Wide Web, as created by Tim Berners-Lee, grew from a tool used by a handful of scientists to a global network that has changed the way people live, work, and communicate.

By the mid-1990s, the web was rapidly expanding beyond academic and research institutions, driven by the rise of new browsers like Mosaic and Netscape Navigator. The explosion of commercial interest in the web led to the creation of countless new industries, from e-commerce to online media.

Berners-Lee's work also had profound social implications. The web democratized access to information, giving people from all corners of the globe the ability to share knowledge, collaborate, and connect in ways that were previously unimaginable. It leveled the playing field, enabling small voices to be heard on a global scale, and it opened the door to innovations like social media, online education, and the gig economy.

Conclusion: A Visionary's Regret

Tim Berners-Lee's creation of the World Wide Web was a groundbreaking achievement that has shaped the modern world. His vision for a decentralized, open platform for sharing information remains one of the most significant technological advances in history. Yet even the most visionary innovations are not without their flaws. The inclusion of the double slashes in URLs is a small but telling example of how early decisions can have far-reaching consequences.

In the chapters to come, we'll continue to explore how the web evolved from these early beginnings, the cultural impact of Berners-Lee's work, and how one small regret serves as a reminder that even the most revolutionary inventions can be refined. The web, like all of technology, is an ever-evolving entity—and understanding its origins gives us insight into how it will continue to shape our future.

Chapter 2: Why the Double-Slash? The Technical Background

The double-slash ("//") in web addresses is a ubiquitous sight, an element so ingrained in our digital experience that most of us hardly question its presence. However, this simple pair of slashes was the result of a specific technical choice made during the early development of the web. In this chapter, we'll explore the deeper origins of the double-slash, its roots in programming conventions, and why, despite its apparent harmlessness, Tim Berners-Lee would later come to regret its inclusion in the URL structure.

The Programming Foundations: Why Slashes Matter

The origins of the double-slash can be traced back to the conventions used in programming languages long before the advent of the World Wide Web. In several coding languages, especially those influential in the 1980s, the double-slash (//) had a specialized meaning: it was commonly used to denote comments or to separate parts of code.

For example:

- In the C programming language, the double-slash ($//$) is used to signify comments, where anything written after the slashes on the same line is ignored by the compiler. This practice helped programmers document their code without affecting its execution.
- In other environments, slashes were also used as separators within file paths, following a similar convention. For instance, UNIX-based systems used the forward slash ($/$) to separate directory names and subdirectory names, forming the hierarchical structure of file systems.

Given these existing conventions, the use of slashes in the Uniform Resource Locator (URL) that Tim Berners-Lee developed was not arbitrary. It reflected the practices of programmers who were used to working in environments where slashes served structural and organizational purposes.

The URL Format: Introducing "http:// "

To understand the inclusion of the double-slash, we first need to grasp the purpose of URLs themselves. Tim Berners-Lee invented the URL as a way to locate and retrieve specific documents on the World Wide Web. It was a breakthrough because it enabled users to access vast amounts of information spread across the internet by typing a simple address into a browser. The structure of the URL was designed to be both human-readable and machine-interpretable.

The basic format of a URL is as follows:

protocol://hostname/path

Let's break this down:

1. **Protocol** – The http (Hypertext Transfer Protocol) at the start of the URL specifies how the data should be transmitted between the user's browser and the server. This protocol was designed to allow the retrieval of hypertext documents—pages linked together by hyperlinks—over the internet.
2. **Double-Slash** – Following the protocol, we find the :// sequence. This sequence is what Berners-Lee would later regret, specifically the double-slash. In its initial conception, it was a separator between the protocol (http) and the hostname, similar to how file paths in computing used slashes to separate directories and subdirectories.
3. **Hostname** – This is the domain name (like www.example.com) which identifies the web server where the requested document is located.
4. **Path** – After the hostname, we have the path to the specific file or document on the server. This also

The Double-Slash Dilemma

uses slashes (/) to signify different directories and subdirectories on the server, following the long-standing conventions of file systems.

Why the Double-Slash? A Practical Inheritance

When Tim Berners-Lee was designing the structure of the World Wide Web in the late 1980s, he had to make several technical decisions based on the systems and conventions available at the time. The inclusion of the double-slash after the protocol in a URL was one such decision, carried over from existing computing practices.

In computing environments of the 1980s, slashes were often used to separate different parts of data structures. For example:

- **File paths** in operating systems, especially UNIX-like systems, used slashes to denote directories and subdirectories, like /home/user/documents/.
- **Network protocols** and other communication formats similarly used slashes as separators, reflecting a hierarchical structure that made navigation and organization simpler.

In this sense, the double-slash (//) following the protocol in URLs was simply an extension of the programming mindset of the era. It was a way to visually and functionally separate the protocol (http) from the rest of the address, providing a clear distinction between the method of access and the specific location of the web resource. It felt natural to programmers and seemed logical in the context of existing systems.

At the time of the web's creation, the inclusion of // posed no obvious downsides. The web was still in its infancy, and its future growth was not yet imagined. The web addresses that contained the double-slash were mostly used by a small number of scientists, researchers, and academic institutions.

A Small Choice with Large Consequences: The Web's Explosion

As the World Wide Web exploded in popularity during the 1990s, the double-slash, a harmless choice in the beginning, started to become a more noticeable inefficiency. The Internet grew exponentially, from hundreds of websites to millions, and eventually to billions. What had initially seemed like a trivial design decision became something that billions of people interacted with daily.

The Double-Slash Dilemma

Each time a URL was typed or shared, the double-slash had to be included, even though it no longer served a meaningful function. The inclusion of these two extra characters began to seem like wasted space—especially as the web began to expand into new devices and formats. For instance:

- **Mobile Devices**: When mobile phones became internet-enabled, screen space was at a premium. Long URLs, including the double-slash, made it cumbersome to display and navigate websites on small screens.
- **Efficiency**: In an age of rapid communication, users appreciated simplicity and speed. The two extra characters seemed like a vestigial element from an earlier time.

What made the double-slash particularly unnecessary was that it didn't affect the functionality of the web. Had Berners-Lee decided to omit the double-slash, the web would have functioned just as well—perhaps even more efficiently. After all, the protocol (http) and the hostname could have been separated by other characters or no characters at all, without any negative impact.

Why Didn't Anyone Remove the Double-Slash?

The Double-Slash Dilemma

By the time the issue of the double-slash became apparent, it was too late to reverse course. The structure of URLs was deeply embedded in the fabric of the web, and changing it would have required a massive overhaul of systems, browsers, and protocols. Furthermore, users had become accustomed to typing http:// at the beginning of web addresses, and removing the double-slash could have caused confusion and incompatibility issues.

In some ways, the double-slash became a symbol of the early days of the web, a small but enduring reminder of the technical choices that shaped the internet's growth. While Tim Berners-Lee may have regretted including it, the fact remains that the World Wide Web's success was not hindered by this design choice. Instead, it serves as a fascinating historical quirk in the development of a technology that changed the world.

A Reflection on the Double-Slash: A Lesson for Future Innovators

The story of the double-slash teaches an important lesson for future technology designers and developers. Even the smallest decisions, those that seem inconsequential at the time, can have far-reaching impacts. The inclusion of the double-slash was a product of its time—an era when programming conventions were carried forward into new systems without fully considering how they might affect the future.

As we continue to develop new technologies, whether it's in software, artificial intelligence, or hardware, the story of the double-slash should remind us to think critically about the decisions we make. Sometimes, the simplest and most elegant solution is the best, even if it means breaking with tradition.

In summary, the double-slash in URLs was not an arbitrary choice, but rather a reflection of the programming conventions that shaped the early internet. While its inclusion didn't hinder the web's growth, it became an inefficiency that Tim Berners-Lee would later regret. Nonetheless, the double-slash remains a testament to the complex interplay between technology, history, and human decisions—proving that even the smallest design choices can leave a lasting legacy.

Chapter 3: The Regret—2009 Reflection on a Small Mistake

In 2009, Tim Berners-Lee, widely regarded as the father of the World Wide Web, made a humble yet fascinating admission. More than two decades after the creation of the web, he publicly expressed regret over a seemingly small but impactful design choice: the inclusion of the double slashes ("//") in web addresses, or Uniform Resource Locators (URLs). To many, this might have seemed like an insignificant detail, but to Berners-Lee, it represented a rare oversight in an otherwise brilliant system. Upon reflection, he realized that the double-slash, so ubiquitous in web addresses, was ultimately unnecessary and could have been left out without any technical drawback. This small decision, though seemingly trivial, had scaled into a global quirk—one that, in hindsight, could have saved billions of keystrokes, time, and even space on our devices.

The Inception of the Double Slash

The story of the double-slash begins in the late 1980s when Berners-Lee was designing the architecture for what would become the World Wide Web. At that time, the internet was already in existence, but it was an arcane system, primarily used by researchers, scientists, and military personnel. The challenge Berners-Lee faced was not just creating the hypertext system itself but devising a way to navigate it—something that could be done simply, reliably, and universally across different types of computers and servers.

When designing the URL, Berners-Lee drew heavily on existing protocols, particularly the File Transfer Protocol (FTP), which was used to transfer files across the internet. In FTP, the double slash served a clear function, delineating the different parts of the address and guiding the computer in finding the correct file on a remote server. As he worked to develop the HTTP (Hypertext Transfer Protocol) standard for the web, he decided to borrow the use of the double slash from older systems.

At the time, this choice seemed logical. It mirrored the structure of existing protocols, was consistent with programming conventions, and didn't appear to present any significant issues. In fact, much of the design of the early web followed the established rules of computing and networking, as Berners-Lee and his colleagues at CERN (the European Organization for Nuclear Research) sought to build on what was already familiar to developers and systems administrators. However, as the web evolved and became a global platform, this tiny design decision would take on far greater significance.

A Matter of Efficiency: The Double-Slash Problem

Fast forward to 2009. By this time, the World Wide Web had grown into an indispensable part of daily life. Billions of people around the world were using the internet for everything from shopping to education, socializing to business. Every day, countless URLs were being typed into browsers, printed in advertisements, written in emails, and shared on social media.

It was in this context that Berners-Lee began to reflect on the decision to include the double slash in URLs. While it had seemed harmless at the time, it now struck him as unnecessary—a relic from an earlier era of computing that no longer served any real function. In an interview with *The New York Times* in 2009, Berners-Lee remarked, "Really, if you think about it, the double slash after the 'http:' in a web address doesn't do anything. It just wastes time and space."

The regret wasn't purely about aesthetics. URLs could be lengthy and cumbersome, and every character mattered. By the late 2000s, people were increasingly using mobile devices to access the web. Typing out web addresses on small, touch-sensitive screens was often frustrating, and any opportunity to reduce the number of characters in a URL could have made a difference in usability.

Moreover, as the number of web pages and URLs grew exponentially, the impact of those two extra characters multiplied dramatically. Each URL required an additional two keystrokes, and while this might not seem significant in isolation, the aggregate effect across billions of web addresses was enormous. In fact, by the time Berners-Lee made his admission, the web had grown to over 100 million websites, and URLs were being typed, clicked, and shared billions of times daily. The cost in terms of time and effort—both for users and systems—was, when scaled, surprisingly substantial.

A World of Screens: The Impact of Small Decisions

In the age of mobile devices, the inclusion of those two extra characters seemed particularly irksome. When the web was first designed, Berners-Lee had not foreseen the rise of smartphones, tablets, and other mobile technologies. The early web was accessed almost exclusively on desktop computers, where screen space was ample and typing on a full keyboard was easy. But by 2009, the shift toward mobile internet use was already well underway, and suddenly, every pixel of screen real estate mattered.

On mobile browsers, URLs were often truncated or displayed only partially to save space, and many people preferred using search engines or bookmarks rather than typing out full web addresses. The double slash, which once went unnoticed on desktop screens, now became a minor but persistent annoyance for mobile users. Every keystroke counted, and any opportunity to streamline the user experience was valuable. Had the double slash been omitted from the beginning, the web might have been just a bit more user-friendly in this new mobile-centric world.

The Accumulation of Small Inefficiencies

Beyond the immediate inconvenience of typing the double slashes, there was also the issue of digital storage and data transfer. URLs are not just typed by users—they are embedded in web pages, linked in emails, printed in documents, and stored in databases. As the number of URLs grew, so did the space required to store them. Every web page on the internet includes links to other pages, and every one of those links contains a URL.

In the grand scheme of things, two extra characters per URL might not seem like much, but when multiplied by the billions of links that existed in 2009—and the trillions that exist today—the total amount of data becomes substantial. Moreover, every time a URL is transmitted across the internet (whether in a web page, an email, or a search query), those extra characters increase the amount of data being sent. In the age of broadband, the impact of a few extra bytes is minimal for most users, but in the early days of dial-up modems, reducing the size of web pages and data transfers was a key priority.

Even today, as the internet continues to expand, data efficiency remains a crucial concern. Cloud storage systems, mobile networks, and content delivery systems all benefit from even small reductions in data size. In this context, Berners-Lee's reflection on the double slash is a reminder that the choices we make in design, no matter how small, can have far-reaching consequences.

Hindsight in Technological Design

Tim Berners-Lee's reflection on the double-slash dilemma offers a fascinating case study in the challenges of technological design. At the time of the web's creation, the inclusion of the double slashes seemed like a logical, even trivial decision. It was consistent with existing protocols, it mirrored file path structures familiar to developers, and it did not appear to introduce any immediate problems. In many ways, it was a decision made in the spirit of practicality and continuity with older systems.

However, as the web grew into a global phenomenon, the small inefficiencies introduced by the double slashes became more apparent. In hindsight, it's easy to see how omitting them might have made the web slightly more efficient, user-friendly, and elegant. But at the time, no one—including Berners-Lee—could have anticipated just how widespread and essential the web would become.

Berners-Lee's admission is a reminder that even the most brilliant inventions are the result of countless decisions, many of them made under conditions of uncertainty. In the fast-paced world of technology, designers and engineers must constantly balance the need for functionality, usability, and innovation, often without fully understanding the long-term consequences of their choices. And as the web continues to evolve, the legacy of those early decisions remains embedded in its architecture.

Conclusion: The Impact of a Small Regret

In the grand scheme of things, Tim Berners-Lee's regret over the double-slash is a minor footnote in the history of the World Wide Web. But it's also a powerful illustration of how even the smallest details can have an outsized impact when scaled globally. While the inclusion of the double slashes did not hinder the web's growth or success, it serves as a reminder that the design of digital systems— no matter how seemingly trivial—can influence the user experience in profound ways.

In the end, Berners-Lee's admission speaks to the humility and foresight of a true innovator. By acknowledging this small oversight, he offers us an opportunity to reflect on the nature of technological progress, the importance of efficiency in design, and the ever-evolving relationship between humans and the digital systems we create.

Chapter 4: How the Web Evolved Despite the Slash

The development of the World Wide Web is one of the most fascinating success stories in modern history. What began as an academic project aimed at improving communication among scientists at CERN grew into the essential framework of today's global digital economy. Central to this evolution was the URL system, which, double-slashes and all, became the gateway to navigating the vast information landscape. While Tim Berners-Lee's decision to include the "//" after "http:" in web addresses was a minor "error" in hindsight, it did not slow the web's growth. Instead, the web continued to flourish, rapidly evolving to become the cornerstone of communication, commerce, and culture.

This chapter delves into how the web evolved in the 1990s and early 2000s, with a focus on the rise of web browsers, the browser wars, the role of the URL system in web navigation, and how search engines revolutionized how users interacted with the internet.

The Early Days: From WorldWideWeb to Mosaic

In 1991, Tim Berners-Lee introduced the first web browser, simply called *WorldWideWeb*. This early browser was both primitive and revolutionary: it allowed users to access text-based documents linked through a network of hypertext links. But this was just the beginning. Although Berners-Lee's invention was groundbreaking, the WorldWideWeb browser had limited capabilities—it only worked on NeXT computers, making it inaccessible to the broader public.

However, the web's next leap forward came with the introduction of Mosaic in 1993. Developed by Marc Andreessen and Eric Bina at the National Center for Supercomputing Applications (NCSA), Mosaic was the first web browser to combine text with graphics, allowing users to view images alongside text on the same web page. This seemingly small change had an enormous impact. Suddenly, the web became much more engaging, intuitive, and user-friendly.

Mosaic was also notable for being available on multiple platforms, including Windows, Mac, and Unix. This cross-platform compatibility dramatically expanded the reach of the World Wide Web, making it accessible to a much larger audience. By late 1993, the web had begun to shift from being an academic tool to becoming a platform that was available to the general public.

At this stage, URLs were still a crucial part of accessing web content. To visit a website, users would type the complete URL into the browser's address bar, including the protocol identifier ("http:"), the double slashes ("//"), and the domain name (e.g., "www.example.com"). The double-slash was not questioned, as most early users were familiar with similar structures from programming or directory paths in their computer systems.

The Netscape Revolution and the Browser Wars

In 1994, Mosaic's success led to the creation of Netscape Navigator, a more advanced browser co-founded by Marc Andreessen. Netscape Navigator quickly became the dominant web browser, celebrated for its speed, ease of use, and enhanced functionality. For the first time, the web was truly open to everyday users, not just scientists or programmers. Netscape made it possible for people with little technical knowledge to navigate the web seamlessly, marking the beginning of the commercial web era.

Netscape's rise also marked the start of the "browser wars." In 1995, Microsoft launched its own web browser, Internet Explorer, as part of the Windows 95 operating system. This bundling of Internet Explorer with Windows played a significant role in spreading web access to millions of homes and businesses. The battle between Netscape and

Internet Explorer for market dominance spurred rapid innovation in browser technology, with each company striving to offer more features and better performance.

Throughout this period, URLs—and the double-slash in particular—remained a key element of web navigation. Users learned to enter "http://" followed by the website's address, and while some may have found the extra characters redundant, they became an accepted part of the web's architecture. As browsers evolved, they began to automate some of these steps. For example, modern browsers would automatically add the "http://" prefix, sparing users from typing it in manually.

Nevertheless, this automation did not eliminate the double-slash. Despite being superfluous, it persisted because changing it would have required a fundamental alteration to the web's underlying architecture. By this time, billions of web pages had already been created, all using the same URL format. Any attempt to remove the double-slash would have caused widespread disruption, and so it remained part of the internet's DNA.

How Users Adapted to the Cumbersome URLs

As the web expanded and users grew more accustomed to navigating it, the somewhat cumbersome nature of URLs became more apparent. URLs could be long and complex, especially when visiting deep pages within a site or accessing specific documents. The presence of seemingly unnecessary elements, such as the "http://" prefix and the double slashes, was a mild frustration for some users, but they adapted.

In the mid-1990s, most users would memorize or write down the URLs of their favorite sites. Typing out full web addresses was common practice, and the inclusion of the double-slash became second nature. At the same time, web developers began to recognize the need for simplicity and user-friendliness. This led to the creation of shorter, more memorable domain names, designed to make web navigation easier.

However, the complexity of URLs persisted, especially as websites grew more dynamic and interactive. URLs could include long strings of characters to represent different pages, parameters, or queries. This made typing out addresses even more challenging, prompting developers to experiment with ways to simplify the process for users.

The Rise of Search Engines: Reducing Dependence on URLs

While users were adapting to URLs, a technological revolution was taking place in the background: the rise of search engines. In 1994, WebCrawler became the first search engine to index the full text of web pages, followed by others like Lycos and AltaVista. But it was Google, founded in 1998, that fundamentally changed how users interacted with the web.

Google's powerful search algorithm made it unnecessary for users to remember or manually type long URLs. Instead, they could simply enter keywords or phrases related to the information they sought, and Google would deliver relevant results. This shift greatly reduced the need for users to interact directly with URLs, allowing them to bypass the cumbersome process of typing out addresses altogether.

As search engines became more sophisticated, they began to dominate web navigation. By the early 2000s, most users no longer needed to know the exact URL of a website—they could simply search for the site or the information they wanted and click on a link. This development significantly minimized the impact of the double-slash, as fewer users were directly entering URLs into their browsers.

URLs and the Modern Web: Hiding Complexity

As the web continued to evolve, web browsers became more adept at hiding the complexity of URLs. Modern browsers like Google Chrome and Mozilla Firefox often automatically hide parts of the URL that are not essential for the user to see, such as the "http://" prefix. The focus shifted to displaying just the domain name, making it easier for users to understand where they were on the web.

At the same time, URLs became even more complex under the hood. The rise of dynamic content, user-generated data, and interactive websites meant that URLs often included long strings of characters representing session IDs, queries, and other parameters. However, for the average user, this complexity was invisible. Modern browsers, combined with search engines and autocomplete features, meant that users could navigate the web without needing to deal with the intricacies of URLs at all.

While the double-slash still exists in most URLs, it is rarely noticed by users today. It has been subsumed into the background of the web experience, a relic of the early days of the internet that persists but no longer holds the significance it once did.

Conclusion: The Web's Evolution and the Endurance of the Double-Slash

The evolution of the web has been marked by rapid technological advancements, user-friendly innovations, and increasing automation. The double-slash, while an artifact of early web design, has had little impact on the web's growth and success. It remains a quirky detail in the history of the internet—an unnecessary yet harmless feature that serves as a reminder of how small decisions can shape the trajectory of major technological innovations.

As the web continues to evolve, with new technologies such as voice search, AI-driven interactions, and decentralized web systems on the horizon, the double-slash may one day fade into obscurity. But for now, it remains a symbol of the web's early days—a mark of both the genius and imperfection that defined its creation.

Chapter 5: The Cultural Impact of URLs

The Uniform Resource Locator (URL), though originally created as a technical tool to help people find information on the World Wide Web, quickly became much more than a string of text in a browser bar. It evolved into a cultural artifact—a symbol of the digital age and a reflection of how the internet has embedded itself into the fabric of daily life. In this chapter, we explore the cultural impact of URLs, how they have shaped the way we interact with brands, movements, and information, and how their design has influenced our relationship with the digital world.

The Rise of URLs as Cultural Icons

In the early days of the internet, URLs were often seen as gateways to exciting new spaces on the World Wide Web. They were more than just technical addresses—they became identifiers, much like physical street addresses, that pointed to destinations filled with information, entertainment, or services. As the internet expanded, specific URLs gained prominence and became synonymous with the brands, services, and communities they hosted. Just like memorable phone numbers or street addresses, web addresses became essential for people to connect with organizations, products, and information.

Some URLs took on a life of their own, becoming symbols of entire digital movements or empires. For instance, **amazon.com** grew from being an online bookstore to one of the most recognized brands globally, representing not just a marketplace but an entire ecosystem of services. Similarly, **google.com** became more than a search engine—it became a verb, "to Google," reflecting its central role in everyday digital interactions. **yahoo.com**, in its early years, symbolized the excitement and vast potential of the nascent internet, offering one of the first major portals where users could access news, email, and a directory of the web.

These web addresses became cultural icons, much like famous company logos or jingles in traditional media. They were easy to remember and inherently linked to the organizations they represented. In some cases, the domain names themselves became valuable assets, with companies paying huge sums to acquire specific URLs that would help define their brand and establish their online presence. The value of a short, simple, and memorable domain name skyrocketed, reflecting the growing importance of the web in business and marketing.

URLs in Everyday Language

As URLs became commonplace, they began to enter everyday language. Phrases like "dot-com" became shorthand for internet-based businesses, as in "dot-com boom" and "dot-com crash," referring to the rise and fall of internet startups in the late 1990s. The term ".com" itself became synonymous with the web, despite the existence of many other domain suffixes like ".org" and ".net."

The inclusion of URLs in advertising—whether on TV, radio, or print—became standard. Brands would prominently display their web addresses, sometimes even encouraging viewers to "visit us online at www.example.com." This further embedded URLs in public consciousness as a central component of brand identity.

Over time, specific URLs began to replace traditional contact methods, such as phone numbers or physical addresses, in advertisements and business communications. Rather than providing a customer service hotline or a mailing address, companies would direct users to their website, reflecting the shift toward online interaction as the primary way people engaged with brands and businesses. URLs became trusted gateways for consumers seeking information, customer support, or products.

URLs also contributed to new internet-based subcultures. The rise of specific web communities, such as **reddit.com**, **tumblr.com**, or **4chan.org**, created a whole lexicon of in-jokes, memes, and shared experiences centered around those websites. These URLs were not just addresses but represented entire social ecosystems, influencing the way users communicated and the types of content that thrived within them.

The Hidden Complexity of URLs

While URLs initially played a visible role in shaping our digital landscape, over time, their technical elements became less prominent in users' daily interactions. The original form of URLs, with the **"http://"** protocol identifier followed by the **"//"** and the domain name, became cumbersome as the web matured. Typing out a full URL, particularly on mobile devices or other platforms with limited input space, was inefficient. Users began to rely more on search engines and bookmarks, which reduced the need to remember or manually enter web addresses.

Modern web browsers responded to this shift by hiding much of the URL's complexity. They began to auto-fill parts of the web address, such as the **"http://"** or **"https://"** protocols, and often did away with displaying the **"www."** prefix altogether. In many cases, simply typing the domain name or the relevant keywords into the browser's address bar would take users to the correct website. This streamlining reflected a growing desire to make the web more user-friendly and to remove the need for users to deal with the technical nuances of URLs.

The rise of **URL shortening services** such as **bit.ly** and **tinyurl.com** also contributed to this trend. As social media platforms, particularly Twitter, imposed character limits on posts, lengthy URLs became impractical. URL shorteners allowed users to condense long web addresses into more manageable and shareable links. This innovation made it easier to share content across platforms, but it also distanced users from the original URL structure, further emphasizing the shift from URLs as visible entities to invisible utilities in the background.

Even today, web browsers like Google Chrome, Mozilla Firefox, and Apple's Safari continue to downplay the importance of full URLs, showing only the core domain (e.g., "amazon.com") in the address bar, while hiding longer or more complex strings like query parameters, subdomains, or protocols. This has made the user experience more seamless but has also removed some of the transparency that early web users experienced when navigating the internet.

The Changing Role of URLs in the Mobile Era

The rise of mobile internet access significantly impacted the way users interact with URLs. On smartphones and tablets, where screen space is limited, displaying long and complex web addresses became impractical. Mobile browsers began stripping down URLs even further, often auto-completing or predicting entire web addresses as users typed. In mobile environments, apps and search engines often served as gateways to the web, meaning users relied less on manually entering URLs.

Apps themselves introduced another layer of abstraction from URLs. Instead of navigating to a website via a traditional address, users would open an app that provided the same services without the need to see or use a URL at all. For example, instead of going to **facebook.com** in a browser, most users would access Facebook through the dedicated app. Similarly, shopping on Amazon or reading news on The New York Times could be done entirely within apps, bypassing the need to interact with URLs altogether.

This shift represented a broader trend toward **"walled gardens"** in which content and services are contained within specific platforms or apps, further reducing the visibility of URLs. While users still relied on the web's underlying infrastructure, they no longer needed to engage directly with web addresses in the way they had in the past.

The Future of URLs: Will They Become Obsolete?

As web technologies evolve, there is a growing question about the future role of URLs. With the rise of voice-activated assistants like Amazon's Alexa, Google Assistant, and Apple's Siri, the way users interact with the web is changing yet again. Instead of typing or even tapping URLs, users can now speak commands like, "Find the best Italian restaurant near me," or "Order toothpaste from Amazon." These voice-activated searches rely on sophisticated algorithms to navigate the web, bypassing the need for users to interact with URLs at all.

The concept of a **decentralized web**, often referred to as Web3, also challenges the traditional role of URLs. In a decentralized web, content might be hosted on distributed networks rather than centralized servers, and URLs as we know them today might be replaced by more fluid, dynamic addressing systems. Blockchain technologies and decentralized identifiers could create a web where users access content through peer-to-peer connections, and the need for static domain names could diminish.

While URLs are unlikely to disappear entirely anytime soon, their role in everyday digital interactions is certainly evolving. The cultural significance of URLs will likely continue to fade as they become less visible and less important to the average user. Instead, search engines, apps, and smart assistants may take over as the primary interfaces for accessing the web, making URLs an invisible but essential part of the underlying infrastructure.

Conclusion: URLs as Cultural and Technical Bridges

Despite these changes, URLs remain a vital part of the web's architecture. They have shaped how we think about digital spaces, how we interact with brands and information, and how we navigate the vast resources of the internet. From their early days as visible, memorable symbols of digital destinations to their current role as mostly hidden technical tools, URLs have played an essential role in bridging the gap between users and the vast information available online.

In the future, even as URLs become less visible, their cultural legacy will endure. They represent a foundational moment in the history of the web, when the need for human-readable, memorable addresses was essential for guiding users through the new frontier of the internet. Although technology may evolve to reduce our reliance on URLs, their impact on web culture, business, and communication is undeniable.

Chapter 6: The Minimalist Internet—What Could Have Been?

Tim Berners-Lee's regret about adding the unnecessary double-slash ("//") in web addresses prompts us to consider a fascinating alternate reality: What if this seemingly minor design choice had never been made? Could the absence of these two characters have altered the trajectory of the internet? In this chapter, we will explore the implications of a more streamlined, minimalist web, considering both the immediate and long-term impacts of omitting the double-slash in URLs. Furthermore, we'll investigate how evolving web technologies, such as mobile apps, QR codes, and smart assistants, are already pushing us toward a future where typing URLs may become obsolete altogether.

The Double-Slash Dilemma: A Reflection on Simplicity

Before delving into the alternate history of the web, it's worth understanding why the double-slash existed in the first place. In the early days of web design, Tim Berners-Lee followed established programming conventions, and the double-slash was a familiar symbol from existing computer systems. In file paths and programming languages, the double-slash served various functions, often used to signify comments or directories. When creating the URL structure for the World Wide Web, it seemed natural to include the double-slash as part of the syntax, even though it had no functional purpose in web addresses.

Looking back, Berners-Lee himself admitted that the double-slash could have been left out without affecting the web's functionality. By eliminating these two characters, the web could have been simpler from the start. The URL, an integral part of navigating the internet, would have been easier to type, read, and share. But beyond the individual convenience of typing fewer characters, the removal of the double-slash may have had broader consequences for how we interact with the internet.

An Alternate History: The Minimalist Web

Let's imagine a world where Berners-Lee opted to exclude the double-slash from URLs, embracing a minimalist approach to web design. Instead of the standard http://www.example.com, web addresses would look more like **http:example.com**. This small change would have saved billions of keystrokes over time, particularly as the internet grew from a few dozen websites to millions, then billions of domains.

In this alternate history, a streamlined URL structure might have influenced the way people perceived and interacted with the web. Shorter URLs would have made web addresses easier to remember, reducing reliance on search engines for navigation. Users could have more easily shared links verbally, reducing the likelihood of miscommunication or typographical errors. Imagine a world where giving someone a website address over the phone or in conversation was as easy as sharing a name or phone number.

The benefits of simplicity in technology are often underestimated. In the realm of user experience (UX), minimalism is highly valued. A simplified URL structure could have set the tone for the entire development of web technology, encouraging a design philosophy focused on reducing unnecessary complexity. This might have led to more intuitive browsing experiences and, possibly, even simpler coding practices for web developers.

Impacts on Web Growth and Efficiency

Could the absence of the double-slash have changed the course of web development at scale? The cumulative savings in time, effort, and cognitive load could have been significant, especially considering the exponential growth of the internet. By eliminating the double-slash from the start, the following areas may have seen long-term improvements:

1. **Typing Efficiency**: Billions of users spend countless hours typing web addresses into browsers, whether on desktops or mobile devices. While the time saved per user may seem small—perhaps a fraction of a second—the global savings could be substantial when multiplied by billions of interactions over decades. Moreover, in environments where bandwidth or data input is limited (such as early mobile phones or low-bandwidth regions), even small efficiencies can have an outsized impact.

2. **Data Storage**: Every web address is stored, transmitted, and indexed across countless servers worldwide. Reducing URL length, even by two characters, could have meant a significant reduction in data storage requirements, particularly in the early days of the web when every byte mattered. While this may seem trivial today in the age of massive cloud servers, storage efficiency was a critical concern in the 1990s and early 2000s.

3. **Screen Space**: In today's mobile-first world, where screen real estate is limited, every pixel counts. A shorter URL would have meant slightly more room

for the actual content of web pages, potentially leading to cleaner, more efficient web designs. This would have been particularly beneficial in the early 2000s, when screen sizes were smaller, and mobile browsing was in its infancy.

4. **International Impact**: The complexity of web addresses can be even more pronounced in regions where English isn't the primary language. In countries where internet users must toggle between different character sets or alphabets, minimizing unnecessary symbols in URLs could have made web navigation more accessible and user-friendly.

The Rise of Alternatives: QR Codes, Mobile Apps, and Smart Assistants

As the web matured, technologies evolved that further minimized the need for manual URL entry, regardless of whether the double-slash remained. These innovations highlight a broader trend toward convenience and user-centered design, moving away from complex, text-based inputs toward more seamless and automated ways of accessing information.

1. **QR Codes**: Quick Response (QR) codes have become a popular way to quickly access web content without the need to type a URL. By simply scanning

a code with a smartphone, users are directed to a web page instantly. QR codes gained traction in marketing, retail, and event spaces, offering a bridge between the physical world and digital information. In a way, QR codes represent the ultimate minimalist web interface—users don't need to remember or type a single character.

2. **Mobile Apps**: The rise of mobile apps further reduced the need for traditional URLs. Instead of navigating through a web browser, users could interact with services directly through dedicated apps, where the underlying URLs are hidden from view. Apps provided a more user-friendly, task-oriented experience, which was especially useful for frequent or repetitive interactions with certain services (e.g., banking, social media, and shopping). In this context, the need for users to understand or interact with URLs became almost obsolete.

3. **Voice-Activated Web Access**: With the advent of smart assistants like Apple's Siri, Google Assistant, and Amazon's Alexa, voice search has become a key driver of web interaction. Rather than typing out URLs or even using QR codes, users can simply speak commands like "Find the nearest coffee shop" or "Open YouTube," and the assistant does the rest. This voice-driven interface reflects the ongoing shift toward a more natural and intuitive way of

interacting with the web, where the complexities of URL structures are increasingly irrelevant to the average user.

The Future of Web Navigation: Toward URL Obsolescence?

As we move deeper into the 21st century, it's worth asking: Are URLs becoming obsolete? The advent of technologies like artificial intelligence (AI), augmented reality (AR), and blockchain-based systems like Web3 suggest that the future of the web may look vastly different from what Berners-Lee originally envisioned. These emerging technologies are pushing the boundaries of how we access and interact with the internet, often bypassing the need for traditional text-based URLs entirely.

1. **AI-Driven Personalization**: AI is transforming how we access web content by anticipating user needs. Smart algorithms now predict what content users are likely to want based on past behavior, reducing the need for direct URL entry or even traditional web browsing. As personalization becomes more sophisticated, users will spend less time navigating web pages and more time directly interacting with the content they care about.

2. **Decentralized Web (Web3)**: The rise of decentralized technologies, such as blockchain, introduces new ways to access and manage web data. Web3 envisions a future where users have greater control over their own data, identities, and online interactions. In such a decentralized web, traditional URLs may be replaced by cryptographic addresses or other identifiers that prioritize security, privacy, and autonomy over simplicity.

Conclusion: Minimalism's Lasting Impact on Technology

The double-slash dilemma serves as a reminder of the power of minimalism in technology. Small design decisions can have lasting consequences, shaping not just the way we interact with systems but also the future direction of innovation. While the double-slash in URLs may seem like a minor issue in hindsight, it symbolizes a larger lesson: The more streamlined, intuitive, and user-friendly we make our technology, the more it enhances our ability to communicate, create, and explore.

As we look to the future, it's clear that the concept of the minimalist internet is already taking shape. Technologies like QR codes, mobile apps, and smart assistants are minimizing the need for traditional URLs, pushing us toward an era where accessing the web is more intuitive and less reliant on manual input. In this sense, the minimalist vision of the internet—where every unnecessary detail is stripped away—has always been the natural direction of progress, with or without the double-slash.

In this imagined alternate history and future, we see that even the smallest design choice, like the inclusion of a double-slash, can reverberate throughout the digital age. While it's impossible to know how things might have turned out differently, reflecting on these decisions offers valuable insights into the importance of simplicity, efficiency, and foresight in technology design.

Chapter 7: The Legacy of Tim Berners-Lee and the Future of the Web

Tim Berners-Lee's invention of the World Wide Web is one of the most impactful technological innovations of the 20th century. His work not only laid the foundation for a new era of global communication and information exchange but also shaped the way we live, work, and interact in the digital age. While the double-slash (//) in URLs is one of his minor regrets, it pales in comparison to the vast influence of his broader vision for the web. This chapter explores Berners-Lee's legacy, the challenges facing the web today, and the potential future of the internet in an increasingly complex digital world.

The Vision: An Open, Decentralized Web

From the outset, Berners-Lee had a clear and ambitious vision for the World Wide Web: it was to be a decentralized platform that would allow anyone, anywhere, to share information freely and easily. His goal was not just to create a new way to communicate but to democratize access to knowledge and provide a platform for collaboration on a global scale. Unlike proprietary systems, which were closed and controlled by corporations or governments, the web was to be an open space where users could navigate, contribute, and innovate without significant barriers.

This vision was revolutionary. Before the web, digital communication and data-sharing were fragmented and siloed. Different systems operated on different protocols, making it difficult for users to connect or share information seamlessly. Berners-Lee's invention unified these disparate networks, creating a universal system that anyone could use.

Central to his vision was the principle of non-discrimination. In other words, the web should not privilege certain users, content, or technologies over others. This idea of "net neutrality" was critical to the web's early growth and remains a contentious issue today. Berners-Lee believed that for the web to fulfill its potential, it had to remain a space that encouraged innovation from the ground up—a "web for everyone."

The World Wide Web Consortium (W3C) and Its Role in Shaping the Web

In 1994, just three years after the launch of the first web browser, Berners-Lee founded the World Wide Web Consortium (W3C). The W3C is a global standards organization that plays a crucial role in the development and governance of the web. Its mission is to ensure that the web remains open, accessible, and interoperable across different platforms and devices.

One of the key functions of the W3C is to establish technical standards and protocols that allow the web to function smoothly. These include standards for HTML (the language used to build web pages), CSS (for styling web pages), and other technologies that enable features like multimedia, interactivity, and security on the web. The W3C's work ensures that developers around the world have a common framework to build upon, promoting a consistent and user-friendly experience for web users everywhere.

For Berners-Lee, the W3C was an extension of his commitment to the web's openness. It was a way to safeguard the web from becoming fragmented or dominated by a few powerful entities. Through the W3C, he sought to establish governance mechanisms that would keep the web free from proprietary control, ensuring that it continued to serve the public good rather than corporate interests.

The W3C also advocates for user privacy and data sovereignty. As the web grew, concerns about data security, surveillance, and user privacy became increasingly prominent. The W3C has been instrumental in developing protocols that protect user information while maintaining the web's open nature. Tim Berners-Lee's advocacy for stronger privacy protections is deeply intertwined with his vision for a web that empowers users rather than exploiting them.

The Rise of Corporate Influence and the Battle for the Open Web

While Berners-Lee's vision of an open and decentralized web has shaped its development, the web has also become a battleground for competing interests, particularly with the rise of powerful tech corporations. Today, a small number of companies—such as Google, Facebook (now Meta), Amazon, and Apple—exercise significant control over vast portions of the web's infrastructure, content, and services. These companies have built highly profitable business models based on user data, targeted advertising, and monopolistic control over key areas of the digital economy.

The rise of corporate influence presents a direct challenge to the ideals Berners-Lee has championed. In recent years, he has become increasingly vocal about the dangers of allowing a few corporations to dominate the web. One of his primary concerns is that these companies prioritize profit over the public good, leading to issues such as:

- **Data privacy violations**: Large corporations often collect vast amounts of personal data from users, using it for advertising and other commercial purposes. This practice raises serious ethical concerns about user privacy and consent.

- **Centralization of power**: The concentration of digital services in the hands of a few companies threatens the web's decentralized structure. As more people rely on platforms like Facebook or Google to access information, these companies gain disproportionate influence over the content and services available online.
- **Algorithmic bias**: The algorithms that power search engines, social media, and content recommendation systems can have a profound impact on what information people see. This creates the risk of echo chambers, misinformation, and the manipulation of public opinion.

Berners-Lee's Response: The Solid Project and Data Sovereignty

In response to these growing concerns, Berners-Lee has embarked on a new project aimed at reclaiming the original values of the web. This initiative, known as **Solid** (derived from "social linked data"), is designed to give users control over their own data. The idea behind Solid is to allow individuals to store their personal information in decentralized "pods" that they control, rather than handing it over to large corporations.

Solid represents a radical shift in how data is managed on the web. Under the current system, users typically relinquish control over their data in exchange for access to services. Companies then use this data to generate profit, often without users' explicit consent or understanding. With Solid, users could choose where their data is stored and who has access to it. This would allow individuals to retain ownership of their digital identities while still participating in the digital economy.

If successful, Solid could dramatically reshape the web, restoring some of the balance of power between users and corporations. It's an ambitious project, but it reflects Berners-Lee's ongoing commitment to ensuring that the web remains a space where individuals, rather than corporations, are in control.

The Future of the Web: Challenges and Opportunities

Looking ahead, the web faces several critical challenges that will determine its future. As new technologies such as artificial intelligence (AI), blockchain, and the Internet of Things (IoT) emerge, the web will continue to evolve in unpredictable ways. Here are some of the key issues that will shape the web's development in the coming years:

1. **Artificial Intelligence and the Web**: AI is already transforming the way we interact with the web, from personalized content recommendations to virtual

assistants like Siri and Alexa. However, the increasing use of AI raises questions about transparency, bias, and accountability. How can we ensure that AI systems are fair and unbiased, especially when they are used to filter information on the web? Berners-Lee has expressed concern about the potential for AI to deepen existing inequalities and reinforce the dominance of tech giants that control vast amounts of data.

2. **Blockchain and Decentralization**: Blockchain technology offers the potential to create a more decentralized web, often referred to as "Web3." By using blockchain to distribute control over data and services, proponents argue that Web3 could reduce the power of centralized platforms and give users more control over their digital identities. Berners-Lee is cautiously optimistic about the potential of blockchain, but he has also warned that decentralization alone is not enough; the web must also remain accessible and equitable.

3. **Privacy and Security**: As more of our lives move online, the importance of privacy and security has never been greater. The rise of surveillance capitalism, where companies profit from collecting and analyzing user data, poses a direct threat to individual privacy. Governments around the world are also grappling with the need to regulate data

collection while respecting user rights. Berners-Lee's advocacy for data sovereignty through projects like Solid is one response to these challenges, but ensuring privacy on a global scale will require coordinated efforts from governments, corporations, and civil society.

4. **Monopolization and Digital Inequality**: The growing dominance of a few tech giants has raised concerns about monopolization and digital inequality. As these companies expand their reach, they risk crowding out smaller players and reducing the diversity of voices on the web. Ensuring that the web remains an open, competitive space is critical to its future. Berners-Lee has called for stronger antitrust measures to prevent monopolistic practices and promote competition.

Conclusion: A Web for Everyone

Tim Berners-Lee's legacy is one of visionary innovation and principled advocacy for an open, decentralized, and user-driven web. While the web has evolved in ways he could not have anticipated, his core values—openness, accessibility, and user control—remain as relevant as ever. As the web continues to face new challenges, from AI and blockchain to corporate monopolization and privacy concerns, Berners-Lee's vision provides a guiding light for the future.

The Double-Slash Dilemma

Ultimately, the future of the web depends on the choices we make today. Whether through initiatives like Solid or broader efforts to regulate the tech industry, the path forward will require a collective commitment to preserving the web's founding principles. If we succeed, we can ensure that the web remains a powerful tool for communication, collaboration, and empowerment—a web for everyone.

Chapter 8: What's Next for Web Design? Innovations and Simplifications

The story of the double-slash dilemma serves as a powerful reminder that even the smallest design decisions can have lasting consequences. Tim Berners-Lee's reflection on the unnecessary "//" after "http:" is a prime example of how early choices in web development, even when made with the best intentions, can shape the user experience for decades to come. As we look to the future of web design, it is critical to remember this lesson: simplicity, accessibility, and user-centered design must always be at the forefront of technological innovation.

In this chapter, we will explore the current and future trends shaping the evolution of web design, from minimalist aesthetics to the increasing integration of artificial intelligence (AI) and voice-activated search. We will also dive into the possible future of URLs and whether decentralized technologies like Web3 will redefine the way we navigate the digital landscape. The next 30 years of web development promise to be as transformative as the last, and the decisions we make today will shape how billions of people interact with the web tomorrow.

1. The Shift Toward Minimalist Web Design

One of the most prominent trends in modern web design is minimalism. In contrast to the flashy, text-heavy, and often chaotic websites of the early 2000s, today's web design tends to favor clean, streamlined interfaces that prioritize user experience (UX). This shift is largely driven by the increasing use of mobile devices and the need to optimize websites for smaller screens. Responsive design—where a website adapts to the screen size and capabilities of the device on which it is viewed—has become a standard practice.

Minimalist web design focuses on reducing visual clutter and simplifying navigation. Key features of minimalist design include:

- **Whitespace**: The intentional use of empty space to create focus and improve readability.
- **Flat Design**: A style that uses simple shapes and flat colors, avoiding unnecessary gradients, textures, and 3D effects.
- **Typography as Design**: Minimalist websites often use bold, large typography as a primary design element, drawing attention to key messages without the need for additional graphics.

- **Fewer Pages, Streamlined Navigation**: Websites are moving toward having fewer pages with more straightforward navigation, reducing the number of clicks required to find information.

Minimalism is not just an aesthetic choice—it is also functional. By focusing on simplicity, websites load faster, perform better on mobile devices, and improve accessibility for users with disabilities. The less-is-more approach also aligns with broader trends in digital user behavior, where users expect fast, efficient interactions with digital platforms.

2. Accessibility as a Priority

Another major shift in web design is the growing focus on accessibility. The web is a global resource, and it must be designed to accommodate people of all abilities, including those with visual, auditory, cognitive, and motor impairments. In recent years, there has been increasing pressure on web developers to ensure their websites meet accessibility standards, such as the Web Content Accessibility Guidelines (WCAG).

Accessibility features in web design can include:

- **Screen Reader Compatibility**: Ensuring that websites can be navigated by users who rely on screen readers to interpret and read aloud the content.

- **Keyboard Navigation**: Allowing users to navigate a website using only the keyboard, without the need for a mouse.
- **Color Contrast**: Designing websites with sufficient contrast between text and background to make reading easier for users with visual impairments.
- **Alt Text**: Providing descriptive text for images, which can be read by screen readers or displayed if the image fails to load.

Accessibility is not just a legal requirement in many jurisdictions; it is also an ethical responsibility. By designing with inclusivity in mind, we can ensure that the web remains a resource for everyone, regardless of their physical or cognitive abilities. As we move forward, accessibility will only become more important, especially with the rise of voice-activated interfaces and AI-driven user experiences.

---

3. The Integration of Voice Search and AI

Voice search is rapidly transforming the way people interact with the web. Thanks to smart assistants like Google Assistant, Amazon's Alexa, and Apple's Siri, users are becoming more accustomed to searching the web, sending messages, and performing tasks using their voice. This shift has profound implications for web design, as traditional text-based interfaces must adapt to the conversational nature of voice interactions.

Key challenges in designing for voice search include:

- **Natural Language Processing (NLP)**: Websites need to be optimized for the way people speak, not just the way they type. This requires an understanding of how questions are phrased in natural language.
- **Featured Snippets**: When users search by voice, they are often presented with a single, spoken answer. This has made optimizing content for featured snippets (the text that appears at the top of a search result) more important than ever.
- **Voice-Activated Interfaces**: Websites and apps are beginning to integrate voice commands as part of their interface, allowing users to navigate through content and perform tasks without touching a keyboard or screen.

AI, in general, is also playing a larger role in web design. Machine learning algorithms can personalize a user's experience based on their behavior, preferences, and location. AI-powered chatbots are becoming standard features on websites, providing users with instant customer support and guiding them through processes like shopping or booking appointments.

As AI continues to evolve, it is likely that we will see more adaptive and personalized web experiences. For example, a website could dynamically rearrange its layout or content based on the user's past behavior, providing a tailor-made experience for every visitor. The integration of AI into web design holds immense potential, but it also raises questions about privacy, data security, and the balance between personalization and intrusion.

---

4. The Future of URLs: Are They Here to Stay?

One of the most intriguing questions facing the future of the web is whether URLs, as we know them, will continue to play a central role in web navigation. URLs (Uniform Resource Locators) have been the backbone of the web since its inception, allowing users to directly access specific websites or pages. However, as search engines and smart technologies become more sophisticated, the need for users to manually type or even be aware of URLs may diminish.

Several factors could contribute to the decline of traditional URLs:

- **Search Dominance**: The rise of search engines, particularly Google, has made it less important for users to know the exact web address of a site. Most users now simply type their query into a search bar and rely on the search engine to deliver the right result.
- **Voice Search**: As voice search becomes more prevalent, users are less likely to recite a specific URL. Instead, they ask questions or give commands, and the smart assistant or search engine handles the navigation.
- **QR Codes and Direct Links**: In mobile-first environments, QR codes, deep links, and app integrations have reduced the need for users to interact with URLs directly. A tap or scan can bring a user to the exact page they need without ever seeing the underlying address.

While URLs are unlikely to disappear entirely, their role may shift to being more of a background function. The future could see a web where user behavior, AI algorithms, and contextual information drive navigation, reducing the need for users to interact directly with URLs. This shift would mark a significant change in how we think about web addresses and access to online content.

5. The Promise and Challenge of Decentralized Web Technologies (Web3)

Another potential disruption to the traditional web model is the emergence of Web3 technologies, which promise a more decentralized and user-controlled internet. Unlike the current web (often called Web2), where large corporations control much of the content and infrastructure, Web3 envisions a web built on blockchain technology, where users have more ownership over their data, identities, and online experiences.

Web3 offers several potential benefits:

- **Decentralization**: Instead of relying on centralized servers, Web3 applications run on blockchain networks, reducing the control of any single entity.
- **Ownership of Data**: In Web3, users can own and control their data, deciding how and where it is shared. This could address some of the privacy concerns that have plagued Web2, where personal data is often harvested and monetized by corporations.
- **Smart Contracts**: Web3 applications can use smart contracts, which are self-executing contracts with the terms of the agreement directly written into code. These contracts allow for more secure, automated transactions without intermediaries.

However, Web3 also faces significant challenges:

- **Complexity**: Blockchain technology is still relatively complex and not yet accessible to the average user. Widespread adoption will require significant improvements in user experience.
- **Scalability**: Current blockchain networks, such as Ethereum, struggle with scalability issues, limiting the speed and efficiency of transactions.
- **Regulation**: The decentralized nature of Web3 raises questions about regulation, security, and the potential for misuse. Governments and regulatory bodies are still figuring out how to handle the challenges posed by decentralized systems.

Despite these challenges, Web3 holds the potential to radically reshape the web by giving users more control over their digital lives. As the technology matures, we may see a gradual shift toward decentralized applications, especially in areas like finance (decentralized finance, or DeFi), social media, and digital identity.

---

6. Imagining the Web in 30 Years

Looking ahead to the next 30 years, it is clear that the web will continue to evolve in ways we can hardly imagine today. Some possible developments include:

- **Immersive Web Experiences**: With advancements in augmented reality (AR) and virtual reality (VR), the web may become a more immersive, three-dimensional experience, where users can interact with digital environments in a much more tactile way.

- **Hyper-Personalization**: AI and machine learning could drive hyper-personalized web experiences, where every user sees a unique version of a website tailored to their preferences, behavior, and needs.

- **The End of Websites?**: With the rise of voice search, AI assistants, and decentralized technologies, the concept of a "website" as we know it could change dramatically. Instead of navigating to specific URLs, users might interact with the web through intelligent agents that deliver content, services, and information directly based on user needs and context.

In this future, the decisions made by web designers, developers, and users today will shape how the web continues to evolve. Just as the double-slash became a lasting artifact of the early web, the choices we make in the name of simplicity, accessibility, and innovation will have far-reaching implications.

Conclusion

The future of web design is full of possibilities, from minimalist, accessible designs to the integration of AI, voice search, and decentralized technologies. As we look ahead, the key challenge will be to balance innovation with the needs of users, ensuring that the web remains an inclusive, accessible, and user-centered space for all. The decisions we make today—whether about something as small as a double-slash or as significant as decentralized systems—will define the web for generations to come.

Conclusion: The Power of Small Decisions

At first glance, the double-slash in URLs might seem like an insignificant quirk in the grand history of the internet. It's a mere two characters, after all, and few users ever stop to question why it's there. However, this seemingly trivial design choice embodies a much larger truth about technology and innovation: even the smallest decisions can have an enormous impact on the way billions of people interact with the world.

Tim Berners-Lee's decision to include the double-slash in URLs was rooted in the programming conventions of the time. It was a practical choice that aligned with the established syntax used in various coding languages, particularly file path structures in systems like Unix. At the moment of its creation, the decision seemed logical and harmless. However, as the web grew from a small academic tool into a global infrastructure connecting billions of people, that small design choice became magnified. Berners-Lee himself later reflected on this choice with a sense of regret, recognizing that the double-slash, though inconsequential on its own, represented an inefficiency that had scaled to a global level.

This candid admission from one of the internet's founding figures holds a profound lesson: even the most brilliant inventions are not without their imperfections. Innovation, by its very nature, is an iterative process. It involves making decisions based on the best information available at the time, and sometimes those decisions turn out to have unintended consequences. The story of the double-slash is not just a story about web design; it's a story about how we, as innovators, must continuously reflect on and improve the tools we create.

The Ripple Effect of Small Design Choices

The double-slash "mistake" serves as a reminder that design choices, however minor, have the potential to ripple across vast systems and have long-term consequences. The decision to include or exclude something as small as two slashes in a URL might seem insignificant in the context of a single website, but when that choice is replicated billions of times, it becomes a global standard that affects the experience of every user on the internet.

Over time, this small design decision had real-world implications. It added unnecessary characters to every web address, requiring millions of users to type and process more information than was strictly necessary. This may seem like a small inconvenience, but as the internet grew and became central to nearly every aspect of modern life, the accumulated time, effort, and resources involved in dealing with those extra characters began to add up. In a world where efficiency and user experience are paramount, every keystroke matters, and even minor inefficiencies can scale into significant issues.

This is particularly true in the context of mobile devices and limited screen real estate. With the advent of smartphones, where users often type URLs on tiny keyboards, the inclusion of unnecessary characters becomes more than a mere annoyance—it can affect usability and the overall user experience. Berners-Lee's reflection on the double-slash highlights how small details in design can have disproportionately large effects, especially when they become ingrained in global systems.

The Process of Continuous Improvement

What makes Berners-Lee's reflection so valuable is his willingness to acknowledge a mistake, no matter how small, and consider how things could have been done differently. This humility is a key aspect of true innovation. It's not enough to simply invent something groundbreaking; the greatest innovators are those who are constantly looking for ways to improve upon their creations, learning from their mistakes, and refining their work to better serve the needs of users.

This idea of continuous improvement is central to the evolution of technology. The history of the internet is full of examples of systems, protocols, and designs that were created with the best intentions, only to be later revised or replaced when better solutions emerged. For instance, the early dial-up connections that once defined internet access have since been replaced by broadband and fiber-optic technologies. Similarly, early search engines like AltaVista gave way to more efficient and user-friendly platforms like Google. In each case, the technological landscape evolved as new challenges and opportunities arose, and the creators of these systems adapted accordingly.

Berners-Lee's reflection on the double-slash reminds us that no invention is ever truly "finished." The web, like all technologies, is a living system that continues to evolve, driven by the needs and behaviors of its users. The ability to recognize and address inefficiencies, even seemingly small ones, is what allows technologies to remain relevant and useful over time. By continually refining our systems, we can ensure that they keep pace with the changing demands of the world.

Efficiency, Accessibility, and Human-Centered Design

One of the most important lessons from the double-slash dilemma is the importance of efficiency and accessibility in technology design. As the internet has grown, so too has the need to make it as user-friendly as possible. Early users of the web were often highly technical individuals who understood the intricacies of URLs, file paths, and coding structures. But as the internet became mainstream, it was essential to simplify these systems to accommodate a wider, less technical audience.

In today's digital age, efficiency is everything. Users expect seamless, fast experiences when navigating the web. Technologies that introduce friction—whether through unnecessary characters in a URL or complicated user interfaces—can quickly become outdated or replaced by more streamlined alternatives. The double-slash, while a minor inconvenience, is a reminder that every aspect of technology design should be approached with the goal of minimizing friction and enhancing usability.

This is where the concept of human-centered design comes into play. The most successful technologies are those that prioritize the needs of their users. This means creating systems that are intuitive, efficient, and accessible to everyone, regardless of their technical expertise. Berners-Lee's regret over the double-slash underscores the importance of putting the user experience at the forefront of design decisions. If the needs of users had been fully anticipated from the start, the double-slash might never have been included, and the web could have been a slightly more efficient place as a result.

Learning from Mistakes to Build a Better Future

The story of the double-slash also highlights a broader principle: the importance of learning from mistakes. Every invention is the product of countless decisions, some of which will inevitably be flawed. But what sets great innovators apart is their ability to recognize those flaws and use them as opportunities for growth. Berners-Lee's reflection on the double-slash shows that even the creators of world-changing technologies are not immune to errors, and that acknowledging those errors is a crucial part of the innovation process.

As we look to the future, the lesson from the double-slash is clear: we must always be willing to reexamine our work, question our assumptions, and strive for improvement. In a world where technology is advancing at an unprecedented pace, the ability to learn from mistakes—no matter how small—will be essential in shaping the next generation of innovations.

Berners-Lee's candid reflection serves as an inspiration for future generations of technologists and innovators. It's a reminder that no detail is too small to matter, and that even the most successful inventions can be improved. By embracing a mindset of continuous learning and improvement, we can ensure that the technologies we create today will continue to serve us well into the future.

The Double-Slash Dilemma

In conclusion, the double-slash dilemma teaches us that the power of small decisions should never be underestimated. Every choice we make in technology design has the potential to impact millions—if not billions—of users. As we continue to build the future of the web and other digital systems, we must remain mindful of these small choices, always striving to make the world more efficient, accessible, and human-centered. Just as Tim Berners-Lee did, we must acknowledge our mistakes and use them as stepping stones toward a better, more connected future.

Bibliography

1. "Weaving the Web: The Original Design and Ultimate Destiny of the World Wide Web" by Tim Berners-Lee

Written by the creator of the web himself, this book provides an in-depth look at the birth and evolution of the World Wide Web. It's a foundational text for understanding the context in which Berners-Lee made his famous decisions, including the double-slash.

2. "The Innovators: How a Group of Hackers, Geniuses, and Geeks Created the Digital Revolution" by Walter Isaacson

A comprehensive history of the key figures behind the digital age, from early computing to the internet. It highlights innovators like Tim Berners-Lee, placing his contributions within a broader narrative.

3. "Tubes: A Journey to the Center of the Internet" by Andrew Blum

This book takes readers on a physical journey through the infrastructure of the internet, from data centers to fiber-optic cables, helping readers understand the real-world components behind the web.

4. "How the Internet Happened: From Netscape to the iPhone" by Brian McCullough

A detailed history of the internet's commercial explosion, focusing on the companies and innovations that shaped the web we know today. It provides a business-focused look at web history.

5. "Where Wizards Stay Up Late: The Origins of the Internet" by Katie Hafner and Matthew Lyon

A deep dive into the origins of the internet, focusing on the pioneers at ARPANET, the precursor to the modern internet. It explains the technical and political challenges that led to the creation of the internet.

6. "Code: The Hidden Language of Computer Hardware and Software" by Charles Petzold

For readers interested in the technical aspects behind the web's creation, this book explains how computers and software communicate, providing context for how the web was programmed.

7. "What the Dormouse Said: How the Sixties Counterculture Shaped the Personal Computer Industry" by John Markoff

This book looks at the social and cultural movements that influenced early computing, offering context for the creative thinking that drove the invention of technologies like the World Wide Web.

8. "The Internet of Us: Knowing More and Understanding Less in the Age of Big Data" by Michael P. Lynch

An exploration of how the internet and big data have transformed our relationship with knowledge and information, relevant to discussions about the evolution of web navigation.

9. "The Internet in Everything: Freedom and Security in a World with No Off Switch" by Laura DeNardis

An exploration of the security and governance issues posed by an internet that has become integral to all aspects of life. This book offers a forward-looking view of the challenges facing the web's future.

Acknowledgments

Writing *The Double-Slash Dilemma: The Inventor's Regret in Web History* has been a journey of discovery, reflection, and exploration of a seemingly small yet impactful decision in the history of the World Wide Web. As with any project, this book would not have been possible without the support, guidance, and inspiration of many people along the way.

First and foremost, I would like to express my deepest gratitude to Tim Berners-Lee, whose groundbreaking invention of the World Wide Web transformed our world in ways we are still uncovering. His honesty and willingness to reflect on the smallest aspects of the web's design—like the inclusion of the double-slash—have inspired this book and given me a fresh perspective on the evolution of technology.

I am also thankful to the numerous engineers, developers, and visionaries who have contributed to the growth of the internet, shaping it into the global network it is today. Without their tireless work and innovation, the web would not be the transformative tool it has become.

I would like to thank my editor, for his keen eye, insightful feedback, and unwavering support. Their dedication to refining my ideas and ensuring that this book resonates with both technical and general audiences has been invaluable.

I would also like to acknowledge the countless authors, technologists, and scholars whose work on the early internet, the evolution of the web, and the design of digital spaces have influenced my own writing and understanding. Your contributions continue to enrich our collective knowledge.

To my friends and family, thank you for your patience, encouragement, and belief in this project. Your support has kept me motivated and focused throughout the writing process.

Finally, I want to extend my gratitude to all the readers who are curious about the history of the web and the unintended consequences of innovation. This book is dedicated to all those who appreciate the fascinating complexities that underlie the digital world we navigate every day.

Thank you for joining me on this journey through the history of the internet, one small decision at a time.

Sincerely,

Zahid Ameer
Versatile Indie Author

Disclaimer

The content of this book, *The Double-Slash Dilemma: The Inventor's Regret in Web History*, is intended for informational and educational purposes only. While every effort has been made to ensure the accuracy and reliability of the information presented, the author and publisher do not make any guarantees regarding the completeness or correctness of the material. The views and opinions expressed in this book are those of the author and do not necessarily reflect the views of Tim Berners-Lee or the World Wide Web Consortium (W3C).

This book is a work of non-fiction that aims to provide a deeper understanding of the history of the World Wide Web, its inventor, and the implications of the decisions made during its creation. Any technical details, anecdotes, or historical interpretations are based on publicly available sources and may be subject to further developments or revisions.

The author and publisher are not responsible for any errors, omissions, or actions taken based on the information provided in this book. Readers are encouraged to verify any information independently before making decisions based on the content herein.

The Double-Slash Dilemma

By reading this book, the reader acknowledges that they are using the information at their own discretion and risk.

About me

I am Zahid Ameer, hailing from the vibrant country of India. As an author, ghostwriter, bibliophile, online affiliate marketer, blogger, YouTuber, graphic designer, and animal lover, I have woven my passions into a unique tapestry that defines my life's work.

Born and raised in India, I have always possessed a deep love for literature. With an insatiable appetite for books, I have amassed an impressive collection of around 1,600 titles, predominantly in English. My passion for reading brings me immense joy and serves as a source of inspiration for my writing endeavors.

I have compiled an impressive portfolio of written works as an author and ghostwriter. With a captivating writing style and an innate ability to craft engaging narratives, I bring my stories to life, captivating readers from all walks of life. My wide range of interests and experiences contribute to the richness of my writing, allowing me to connect with my audience on a heartfelt level effortlessly.

Beyond my literary pursuits, I have also established a strong presence on various digital platforms. I utilize my YouTube channel and blog to raise awareness about all types of knowledge and to share heartwarming stories of animals. Using my platform to shed light on important issues, I strive to create a world where humans and animals can coexist harmoniously.

In addition to my work as an author, I have also dabbled in the world of affiliate marketing. With my webpreneur spirit, I have ventured into online marketing, leveraging my knowledge and skills to promote products and services that align with my values.

However, my most cherished role is that of a father. Family is at the core of my being, and everything I do is centered around creating a better future for my loved ones. My dedication to my family is evident in my passion for personal growth and my relentless pursuit of success. Through my various endeavors, I strive to set an example of perseverance and ambition for my children, inspiring them to chase their dreams unapologetically.

In a world where specialization often dominates, I defy convention by embracing multiple passions and excelling in diverse fields. My love for books, animals, and family has become the driving force behind my achievements. By the grace of Almighty God, my unique blend of characteristics has allowed me to leave an indelible mark on the world, enriching the lives of those I encounter along the way.

To your grand success in life,

Zahid Ameer
Versatile Indie Author